D1680997

CREATEST

STAFFORDSHIRE LIBRARY AND INFORMATION

Please return or renew by last date shown

KS

	3. MAY 06	
27. NOV 04	SEP 04	
16. 03. 05	09. 07	
	16. AUG 07.	
02. APR 05.		
	15. OCT 0	
30. APR 05.	10. NOV 07	
DEC 05.		
	05. NOV 08.	
06.	29. SEP 09	
18. APR 06.		

If not required by other readers this item may be renewed, in person, by post or by telephone. Please quote details above and date due for return. If issued by computer, the numbers on the barcode label on your ticket and on each item, together with date of return are required.

24 HOUR RENEWAL LINE - 0845 33 00 740

Sterling Publishing Co., Inc.
New York

To three gifted writers—April, Dianna, and Frances
Love—P.Y.

To Professor Lemaitre and his dedicated staff
at the Laugh-Aroni Institute
—M.R.

STAFFORDSHIRE LIBRARIES ARTS AND ARCHIVES	
38014038270671	
PET	26-Aug-04
827	£3.99
BURT	

Library of Congress Cataloging-in-Publication Data

10 9 8 7 6 5 4 3 2 1

Published by Sterling Publishing Co., Inc.
387 Park Avenue South, New York, NY 10016
© 2003 by Matt Rissinger and Philip Yates
Distributed in Canada by Sterling Publishing
^{c}/o Canadian Manda Group, One Atlantic Avenue, Suite 105
Toronto, Ontario, Canada M6K 3E7
Distributed in Great Britain and Europe by Chris Lloyd at Orca Book
Services, Stanley House, Fleets Lane, Poole BH15 3AJ, England
Distributed in Australia by Capricorn Link (Australia) Pty. Ltd.
P.O. Box 704, Windsor, NSW 2756, Australia

Manufactured in the United States of America

Sterling ISBN 1-4027-0560-3

CONTENTS

WHY DID YOU FINISH THE CEREAL?

What's a Comeback, Anyway?

QUESTION: **How was school today?**

COMEBACKS:

The police will fill you in later.

Aside from the flood, earthquake and fire drill it
was totally boring.

There are no stupid answers to stupid questions—
only great comebacks or, as the dictionary defines
them—"smart retorts."

Comebacks don't have to be insulting (but they
can be, of course!). They can be funny, sarcastic, or
just plain ridiculous. Everyone needs a little playful
banter or an artful dodge now and then. When
you're loaded with a lovely comeback at your ready
disposal, you'll make your friends laugh, your
parents groan, and your teachers send you to
detention (just kidding).

So whether you want to bust a bully, diss your sis, or just encourage people to stop taking life so seriously, this book contains enough comebacks to make you "King or Queen of all Comics."

So what are you waiting for? A royal invitation? It's time for you to make a fabulous comeback!

—Matt and Phil

(By the way, if you memorize enough of these, you might just get an A on your retort card!)

1. COOL SCHOOL CRACK-UPS

Why were you absent yesterday?

I was working on my perfect non-attendance record.

Sorry, the government UFO scientists have sworn me to secrecy.

It was National Show & Tell Day. I didn't show, and that's all I can tell.

I wasn't absent. I was just wearing my new Harry Potter Invisibility Cloak.

Why are you late to class?

Our bathroom tiles needed grouting.

My favorite commercial was on TV.

I've been traded to Cincinnati.

The dog ate my wake-up rooster.

I had to knit some dust bunnies for a charity bazaar.

I'm having my baby shoes bronzed.

I had to go to court for kitty littering.

I was practicing for the math test by counting the bristles in my toothbrush.

I had to jog my memory.

I had to sit up with a sick ant.

My superpowers failed me again.

Is this a quiz?

My foot fell asleep and I didn't want to wake it up.

Why did you bring your snake to school?

It's not a snake, it's a mouse detector.

It's no snake; it's my new battery-operated belt.

It's not a snake — it's my flexible ruler.

I'm viper-active.

Oh that's not a snake—it's a worm with a superiority complex.

Is that your graffiti on the bathroom wall?

That's not graffiti—it's a plea for fluffier toilet paper.

Couldn't be—I always use a purple crayon.

No, it's Egyptian hieroglyphics. There must be a mummy loose in the building.

Yes. Does this mean I won't make Student of the Month?

Is that a calculator?

No, it's a very small first aid kit.

No, it's a cell phone. I'm calling 1-800-Help-Me.

No, it's just a sandwich with a built-in function key.

No, it's a very flat kazoo.

No, I'm really an android, and this is my external power pack.

Yes, and according to my calculations my days are numbered.

No, it's a mind-control device for teachers. Hope you don't mind....

Correct, for one million dollars.

Are your eyes on someone else's paper?

Oh, so that's where they landed!

Yes, but I was only checking for copyright violations.

Absolutely not—never once did my eyes leave my head.

Can't be mine. I always dot my eyes.

No, I was just testing my X-ray vision.

On the paper, no. On the ink, yes!

Must you keep tapping your pencil?

I'm not tapping. The room must be haunted.

Shh! I'm trying to attract birdies for my
"Woodpeckers of the World" report.

I still have three more taps to go, and then it's
Harry's turn.

This is my book report on Morse code.

Sorry, I'll switch to pens from now on.

Yes. I'm trying to send a coded message to the
authorities that I'm being held captive.

How do you think you'll ever get to high school with grades like this?

My stunning good looks, of course.

I try not to think—it gets in the way of my grades.

My uncle owns the bus company.

I'm hoping you'll be so sick of me you'll drive me over there yourself.

2. KNUCKLEHEAD NUTRITION

Are you eating Chinese food?

No, I'm using these wooden sticks as appetite suppressants.

No, it's take-out pizza with stilts.

No, I'm trying to attract beavers with these little wooden sticks.

No, this is Italian food in disguise.

Do you call that lunch?

Yes, but yesterday I used to call it my pet armadillo.

It was fresh at breakfast.

I just serve it. I don't cook it.

It's my new recipe: Garbage à la mode.

Yes, but yesterday I called it road kill.

I'll let you know as soon as the Crime Scene Investigators leave.

No, these big blocks of petrified tofu make great book shelves.

Yes, it's a seven-course meal: A six-pack of Coke and a donut.

Don't you like the food in the school cafeteria?

I like it at times— the times I see it swirling down the garbage disposal.

Are you kidding? The food's so bad even the teachers have food fights.

Is this a trick question?

From what I've heard, even the flies have to see the school nurse.

Interesting vocabulary choice. I wouldn't exactly call it food.

Yup, but I also like scratching my nails on a blackboard.

Maybe it was a typo, but I've been nervous ever since the menu read "Spit Pea Soup."

Yes, but I'm also fond of toxic waste.

Why did you take so much cafeteria food?

I was only trying to protect those who followed me.

I'm a glutton for punishment.

I have to leave now; I can't stomach any more of your questions.

I'm taking it back to science class. Our topic today is unsolved mysteries.

Oh, this isn't cafeteria food. It's what's left over from our frog dissection experiment.

I figure if a bully attacks me the meat loaf will come in handy.

It's the quickest way to see the school nurse and get sent home.

23

Are you going to eat that apple?

Yes, but first I'm having that worm taste test it for me.

Why not? Snow White did.

No, I thought I'd have it bronzed and put in my trophy case.

No, I thought I'd just sit here and watch the seeds germinate.

No, I'm going to teach it to do some cool tricks. Did you ever see an apple turnover?

No, I'm going to sit on it and make sauce.

No, I'm playing William Tell's son in a school re-enactment.

No, I'm going to dry it and make a shrunken head for my dark arts class.

Why aren't you eating our meat loaf?

I am, but strangely it seems to keep regenerating on my plate.

Meat loaf? I thought it was a moon rock.

I don't like to eat things older than myself.

Oh, was that meat loaf? I thought it was corn meal mush.

I thought if I collected enough of these I could make a cool skateboard ramp.

3. RAPID RECOVERIES

Well, after I do all my homework, I'll have just
  enough time to take a shower and get back on
  the school bus.

I have to alphabetize my e-mail spam.

I'm taking all the sponges out of the ocean to see
  how much deeper it gets.

I'm not going to spend it. I'm saving up my days
  for a good mid-week vacation.

I didn't ask a question. Why is your hand up?

I'm testing my new deodorant.

I'm seeing if my new robotic arm unscrews.

Somebody has to catch the flies.

I'm worried the ceiling might fall down.

I'm rehearsing for the part of the Statue of
Liberty in the school pageant.

We're going to New York for a field trip and I was
practicing hailing a cab.

Because you said hands-down I was the least
attentive student in class.

I was just seeing how my nails look from a
distance.

Somebody had to catch the spitball before it hit
you in the face.

Why did you throw that paper airplane?

I'm auditioning for a part as one of the Wright Brothers.

I was just testing your radar.

I was training my pet ant for future space missions.

I'm trying to rack up frequent flyer miles.

My mouth is too dry to make spitballs.

The kid next to me built an anti-aircraft missile and we were just testing it.

It's not an airplane—it's an origami flying fish.

Are you sleeping at your desk?

Why? Did you want to sleep here too?

Yes, but I could lie down in the teacher's lounge, if
you like.

No, my brain just gave out.

Why? Was I snoring again?

No. I'm just researching a paper on dream
   interpretation.

No. Somebody put Super Glue on my arms.

Do you talk back to your parents, too?

No, my dog is a ventriloquist. He speaks for both of us.

No, I'm always up front with them.

I have no parents—Australian dingoes raised me.

No, they talk back to me. That's why we're all
   grounded for a week.

Yes, we're on a family cell phone plan.

No, I come from a family of mimes.

I try, but they can't hear me locked in the closet.

Yes, we love classical music. You did say talk
   Bach, didn't you?

How did you manage to flunk every class?

I owe it all to that new program "Hooked on Stupidity."

Everyone needs a goal.

At least I'm consistent.

Practice makes perfect.

4. MESS ME?

What's your excuse for not taking a bath today?

I'm saving money on the water bill.

We don't have flood insurance.

I took so many baths last week my friends are calling me "Rusty."

Everyone at school says I look cute cruddy.

I think the soap dish is haunted.

Dad accidentally crossed the shower connection with the ice maker.

Didn't I tell you to clean your room?

Yes, but I heard on the news that the president is going to be visiting disaster areas today.

Shh! I think Grandma is lost in my dirty laundry. Let's listen for tapping sounds.

I cleaned it, but my evil twin must have messed it up again.

I'm sorry; I think you have me confused with someone from a parallel universe.

I won't answer any more questions until my lawyer arrives.

Yes, but first you'll have to raise my allowance... renting a bulldozer isn't cheap.

Are those crumbs in your bed?

No, they're alien life forms from planet Twinkie.

No, it's fish food. I'm trying to lure out my goldfish. I lost him among the covers.

Yes, I'm laying out a smorgasbord for the Tooth Fairy.

Oh, my gosh! It's a jail break from my ant farm!

No, I was reading a sad story to my Oreo cookies and they just fell to pieces.

Yes, I just finished making toast with my new electric blanket.

No, sawdust. Lately I've been sleeping like a log.

Well, no wonder I've been feeling so crummy.

Do you think this is a hotel and I am your maid?

No, but you know those neat little soap bars — could you get me some of them?

Yes, and as a matter of fact, I wanted to talk to you about the lack of towels.

Of course not. By the way, what time is check-out?

Of course not. By the way, what time does the pool open?

Does this mean I don't have to tip you?

No, this is Buckingham Palace and you are my butler.

I'll call you later for room service.

Of course not. By the way, my wake-up call is 11 AM.

Actually, it feels more like Frankenstein's castle.

Are you going to mow the lawn?

No, I figured if the grass grew high enough we wouldn't need curtains.

No, I'm trying to get back to my roots.

No, I left the mower out in the yard and now the grass is too high to find it.

No, I'm hoping to adopt a herd of goats soon.

No, I'm trying to create a habitat for my pet giraffe.

No, I thought you said "moo" the lawn. Now what'll we do with all these cows?

No, a truck was just here that said "Lawn Doctor," and I didn't want to disturb the patient.

What are you doing up so late?

I'm doing research on TV infomercials.

The dog is sick, so somebody has to bark at the
   burglars.

I'm already too beautiful for beauty sleep.

If I sleep too long my tongue gets wrinkled.

5. SAY "TOUCHÉ"

Why didn't you take out the recycling bin?

I was waiting for Earth Day.

I took it out, brought it in, took it out, and
brought it in. Recycling is tiring.

I did. I took it out to dinner.

I'm saving the aluminum to build a 747 in the
basement.

How many times do I have to tell you to keep quiet?

Sorry, I wasn't paying attention. Tell me what?

If I guess correctly, do I win a prize?

As soon as we make it into the *Guinness Book of World Records*.

Let me get my calculator.

I'm not sure. We haven't studied this in math class.

Let me finish practicing my bass drum and cymbals and then we can talk.

Hold on...I'm reading your mind. Three thousand?

Does that include my three other personalities?

They say silence is golden, but I've always liked going for broke.

Did you go to Disney World for vacation?

No, these are tiny satellite dishes, not mouse ears.

Yes, we did. Any more Goofy questions?

Yes, since I'm such a big cheese I went to mouseland.

Yes, we went to practice standing in line.

Yes, we came back but our money is still there.

No, I won the billion-dollar lottery so I had Disney World brought to me.

Yes, and my dad's still there in the Donald Duck lot looking for our car.

Is this seat empty?

No, it's half full.

No, and my imaginary playmate will be very
  angry if you sit on him.

That's not a seat—it's my personal exercise area.

Not according to Einstein's theory of relativity.

No, but I'm saving it for my personal bodyguard.

It wasn't empty until I started peeling off my underwear. Be my guest.

Ask the Invisible Man. He's sitting right there.

No, it's a mini-heliport for James Bond.

Other than the wad of gum stuck to it, yes. Go ahead and sit down.

No, according to my science teacher it's chock full of air molecules.

Yes, but be careful. The last kid who sat there got ejected through the roof.

Why don't you want to go along to your sister's ballet recital?

I'm tu-tu tired.

I'm taking up totem pole carving.

I have to fluff my shower cap.

I made an appointment with a cuticle specialist.

My plot to take over the world is just starting to thicken.

I have some real hard words to look up in the dictionary.

I'm giving nuisance lessons at a convenience store.

None of my socks match.

Is that a jigsaw puzzle?

No, I got frustrated and cut up my homework assignment.

It is now, but a few minutes ago it was a ceramic wall hanging.

No, I spilled a box of Corn Flakes.

No, I borrowed the Dead Sea Scrolls from the Museum and look what happened.

Yes, and they're not kidding when they say, "Some Assembly Required!"

6. HA-HA HYGIENE

Is that a battery-powered toothbrush?

No, it's a nuclear-powered toothbrush…Like my glowing smile?

No, it's a mini-sandblaster.

No, it's a battery-powered shoeshine kit. I just put my foot in my mouth.

No, it's a cordless microphone. Karaoke anyone?

No, it's a magic wand for the Tooth Fairy.

Are you sneezing?

No, I'm just road testing a new allergy.

No, I'm learning a foreign language.

No, I'm just flushing my brain.

No, I'm misting the plants.

Are you wearing braces?

Why? Did I set off the metal detectors?

No, they're wraparound magnets that hold my
head together.

No, that's a test track for miniature trains.

No, I absent-mindedly mistook Christmas tinsel
for dental floss.

No, that's the latest mouth fashion from the
Hannibal Lecter Collection.

Why don't you ever flush the toilet?

Why, did someone call the EPA?

I'm afraid the ghost of my long-lost goldfish may flow back.

Watching the water go round and round makes me dizzy.

If I want to see rushing water, I'll visit Niagara Falls.

What do I look like...a plumber?

Is that your real nose?

Yes, and if you stand under it the rain won't touch you.

Yes, and I'm hoping it's big enough to poke a hole in the ozone.

Yes, and it comes with a ski lift.

Yes, would you care to hang up your coat?

Yes, but it is someone else's face.

Are you really on a diet?

Why should I be? I'm the perfect weight for my
   shape, aren't I?

Yes, as soon as I find a gym with a Dairy Queen.

Yes, it's called the Piranha Diet. You jump into
   the lake and lose fifty pounds in ten seconds.

Yes, but only between meals.

Yes, it's called the Banana Peel diet…the pounds
   just slip off.

Why did you cut your hair so short?

Well, that's what you get for putting your head in the clothes dryer.

It'll grow back when the moon is full.

The witness protection program said it would be a good idea.

I pointed to a styling picture, but the barber thought I was pointing at a bottle of Mr. Clean.

I'm going trick or treating as a bowling ball.

Is that your cologne?

Yes, it's called, "Wet Dog."

Are you kidding? I haven't got a scent to my name.

Sorry, I'll put my sneakers back on.

No, I think the plants are wilting because they need water.

7. COMICAL COMEBACKS

No, they put my school yearbook on DVD.

Hey, it's a video from my family reunion.

No, that hairy creature is my Uncle Sal playing baseball.

No, it's a surveillance video from our school cafeteria.

No, it's an exercise video for Tubby Trolls.

Why is your room such a mess?

Did those darn raccoons get in again?

This is my homework project on pig sties.

Well, after the bathroom flooded we had to play here.

I'm sorting my underwear into three categories: The Good, The Bad, and The Ugly.

I'm arranging my gym socks in alphabetical odor.

The family of rats living under my bed refuses to pack up.

I'm trying to create the world's largest indoor landfill.

My doctor says I can't lift anything heavier than a remote control.

What did you learn in school today?

Don't ever start a food fight with an octopus.

My teacher hates finding rubber snakes in her desk drawer.

The principal's office is painted a very calm shade of blue.

When you open the emergency exit door of the school bus, the driver's face turns purple.

Never stick a pencil up your nose for your school picture.

How to pick the lock on the detention door.

Be sure to hide your binoculars when cheating on a test.

Is that a back pack?

No, I'm practicing for the part of the Hunchback of Notre Dame.

No, it's a horrid growth. I'm on my way to the emergency room right now.

No, it's a papoose. Wanna see the cute li'l fellow?

No, it's a parachute. Watch me while I bail out of class.

No, I'm auditioning for that new reality show: "World's Worst Wedgies."

No, it's a rocket pack. Want to take a test ride?

Yes. When I was wearing it around my front, baby kangaroos kept jumping in.

No, I'm giving a piggyback ride to an alien life form.

No, it's a battery pack. I'm feeling a bit run down today.

No, it's a leaf blower. Stand back while I crank this baby up.

No, it's an oxygen tank for that final exam we're taking today.

Is that your dog?

If he bites you he's not.

No, that's my pet ferret—he's going through an identity crisis.

No, my cat always dresses up for Halloween.

No, that's my dad. I was raised by wolves.

No, it's a giant hairball with legs.

No, my sister's a witch and that's what's left of her new boyfriend.

Shh! Not too loud—he thinks he's the world's cleverest hamster.

Are you taking your dog to obedience school?

No, isn't today Take-Your-Pet-to-Work Day?

No, he's taking me. He signed both of us up online.

Yes, I need him to obey the command, "Eat my homework."

Yes, he keeps cutting in line at the fire hydrant.

Yes, he's confused. He keeps chasing bones and
burying sticks.

No, I'm taking him to cooking school. He's tired of
those dry biscuits.

Why can't you sit still?

I am still; it's the earth that's moving.

I'm using my underwear as an ant farm.

I want to get a jump on the door in case we have a fire drill.

I'm practicing for my blurry picture for the school yearbook.

8. ON THE EDGE

Are you playing marbles?

No, these tiny crystal balls let you see the future—but only a little bit at a time.

Marbles! We thought they were ice crystals from the Mesozoic period.

No, we're in a bowling tournament with ants.

These aren't marbles— they're petrified malted milk balls.

How come you're not going to school today?

I'm staying home to work on my cottage cheese sculpture.

It's my parakeet's birthday.

I'm doing door-to-door collecting for static-cling victims.

I'm teaching my ferret to yodel.

I have to check the freshness dates on my dairy products.

I'm going through cherry cheesecake withdrawal.

My crayons need sharpening.

I'm in training to be a household pest.

I'm sandblasting my Easy-Bake oven.

I'm worried about my vertical hold.

I have to go down to the bakery to watch the
bread rise.

My Morris the Cat Fan Club is meeting this
morning.

Why should I increase your allowance?

I'm saving up for a beach house.

My piggy bank went bankrupt.

What allowance? I can't even afford to pay anyone a compliment.

Then you won't have to worry about me digging under the sofa cushions when you're trying to take a nap.

My pet caterpillar needs flying lessons.

Because I'm tired of checking vending machines for spare change.

Are you still talking on the phone?

That's amazing! I'm on the psychic hotline and they predicted you would ask me that!

I'm shooting for a place in the *Guinness Book of World Records*.

Would you believe the handset is stuck to my ear?

Would you rather I fly to Europe than call?

I called a baby and now I'm on crawl waiting.

I'm talking to a mummy and we're just wrapping up now.

I have this hang-up about hanging up.

Is it true your parents grounded you?

No, it's false. The FBI has me under house arrest.

My astrologer told me not to go out until New
   Year's.

Yes, cut off from everything with only my CDs,
   DVDs, TV, PC, and cell phone to keep me
   company.

No, that's an out-and-out lie and as soon as I'm
   allowed to leave my house, I'll set the record
   straight.

No, the doctor wants me to stay at home until I'm
not contagious.

Not really, they just want me home more to talk
to the houseplants.

Nonsense, I can go anywhere I want—like the
living room, den, kitchen—even the garage.

Grounded? No It's more like my house is an
airport and I've only gotten clearance to taxi to
the end of the driveway.

No, I'm just trying out how it feels to be home
schooled 24/7.

Are you jumping on a trampoline?

No, I've stumbled upon the world's smallest earthquake zone.

No, I accidentally cooked Mexican jumping beans for lunch.

No, the moon's gravitational pull is really strong today.

No, I just slipped on a patch of zero gravity.

Quick! Call an ambulance! There's a swarm of bees in my BVDs.

9. CLASSIC COMEBACKS

Is that your mom?

No, that's my boot camp sergeant. He's a pussycat compared to my mom.

Yes, she's hard to recognize without her bullhorn.

No, it's the TV repairman—he has a flair for fashion—wouldn't you say?

Ever have some friends you're just not crazy about? Try these great comebacks the next time they ask you to hang out with them:

I'd like to hang out with you, but...

I'm building a cow from a kit.

I'm attending the opening of my garage door.

I promised to help a friend fold road maps.

I'm trying to be less popular.

I have to study for a blood test.

I have to rotate my crops.

I have to floss my cat.

I promised to spend some time with my imaginary
   playmate.

I did my own thing and now I've got to undo it.

Are you coloring Easter eggs?

No, we're just painting the outside of these mini-chicken coops.

Eggs? Nah, we thought we'd just color and put numbers on these misshapen billiard balls.

Yes, we're coloring them. We tried wallpapering them but it didn't stick.

Yes, my therapist says it will help me come out of my shell.

No, we're dusting these oval objects for fingerprints.

90

Are you doing your homework right now?

I'm doing my homework. Whether it's right or not is up for debate.

No, I thought I'd do someone else's homework.

No, I'm doing it last week. You just traveled back in time.

No, I'm writing a story about someone who always asks stupid questions and ends up turning into a toad.

No, I'm adding up how many times a minute you interrupt me.

Is this goodbye?

I can't say anything. I'm practicing to be a mime.

Yes, I think it's time I leave and annoy someone else.

Yes, the Mother Ship should be arriving any minute now.

No, the pages are just written in invisible ink from here on out.

No, this is hello in a parallel universe!

ABOUT THE AUTHORS

Matt lives near Valley Forge, Pennsylvania, with his wife Maggie, his daughters Rebecca, Emily, and Abigail, and their black Lab, Breaker. Philip lives in Austin, Texas, with his wife Maria and his cats Sam and Johnnie.

Philip and Matt's other Sterling books include *The Great Book of Zany Jokes, The Biggest Joke Book in the World, World's Silliest Jokes, Best School Jokes, Greatest Jokes on Earth, Totally Terrific Jokes, Giggle Fit: Nutty Jokes, Greatest Giggles Ever,* and *It's Not My Fault: Kids' Excuse Book.*

ABOUT THE ILLUSTRATOR

An award-winning cartoonist and author, Jeff Sinclair has illustrated dozens of humorous children's books that are sold all over the world. He lives just outside of Vancouver with his wife Karen, son Brennan, daughter Conner, and a very mischievous golden retriever puppy named Vinnie.

INDEX